HAPPY VALENTINE'S DAY
TO:

Help these kittens get through the maze!

YOU ARE SO PURRFECT!

Connect the dots.
WISHING YOU A VALENTINE'S DAY AS SWEET AS YOU ARE!

Help these two hedgehogs reach each other before Valentine's Day.
I LOVE YOU OODLES AND OODLES!

Color, cut, and glue this bow on another sheet of paper.
YOU ARE A LITTLE LOVE BUG!

Cut & Glue
COLOR
CUT OUT
GLUE
USE EXAMPLE OR YOUR IMAGINATION
1
2
3

**Help this bear get through the maze.
YOU ARE BEARY SPECIAL!**

**Connect the dots and then color the watering can.
YOU ARE WONDERFUL!**

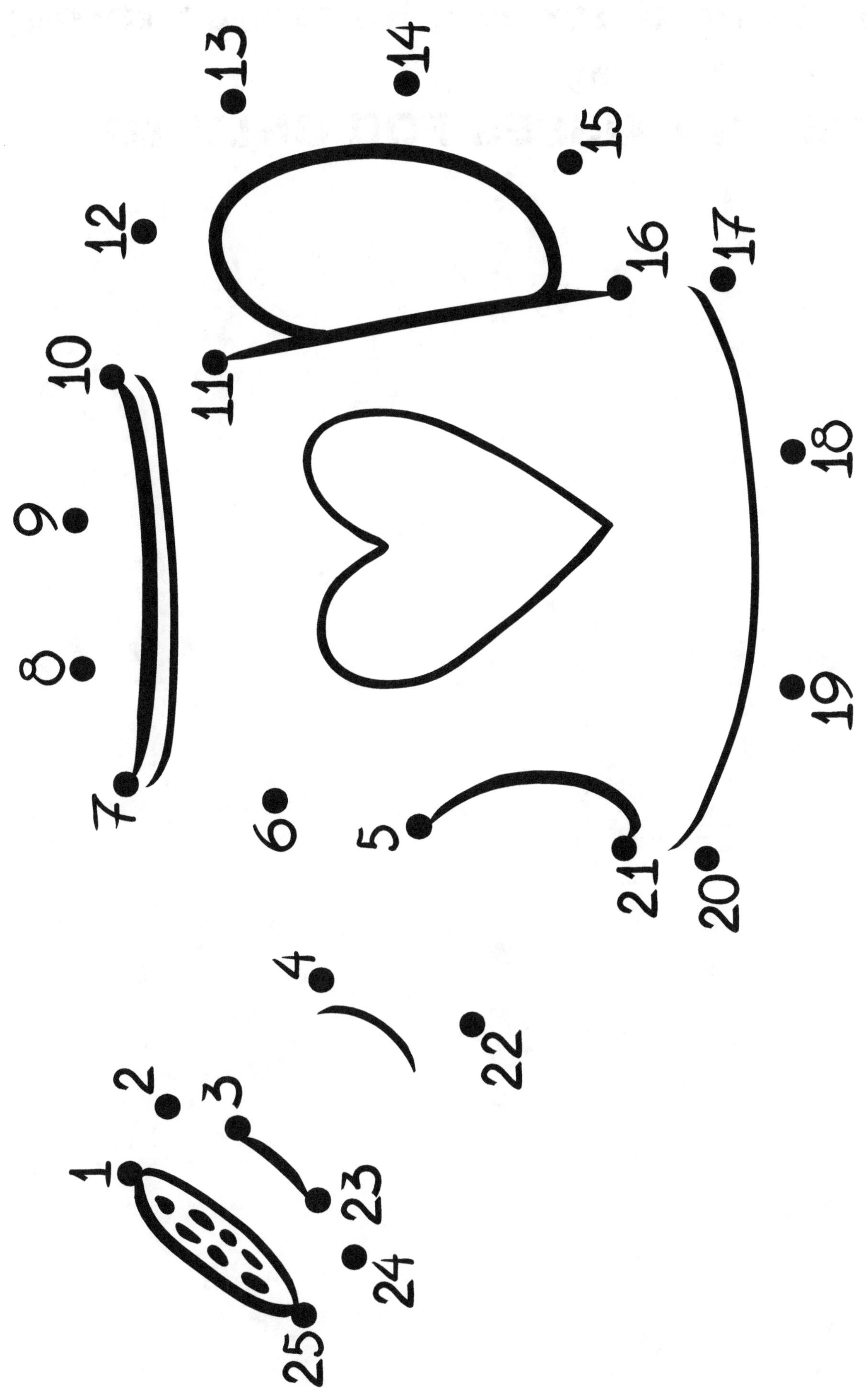

**Reach cupid before she sleeps through Valentine's Day!
HUGS AND KISSES FOR ONLY YOU!**

**Connect the dots and color the hedgehog.
I ONLY HAVE EYES FOR YOU!**

**Color by number.
UR TOO CUTE!**

1 - light blue 2 - dark green 3 - green 4 - yellow
5 - orange 6 - beige 7 - brown 8 - red

Color, cut, and fold the valentine and give it to someone special.

I CANNOT CONTAIN MY LOVE FOR YOU!

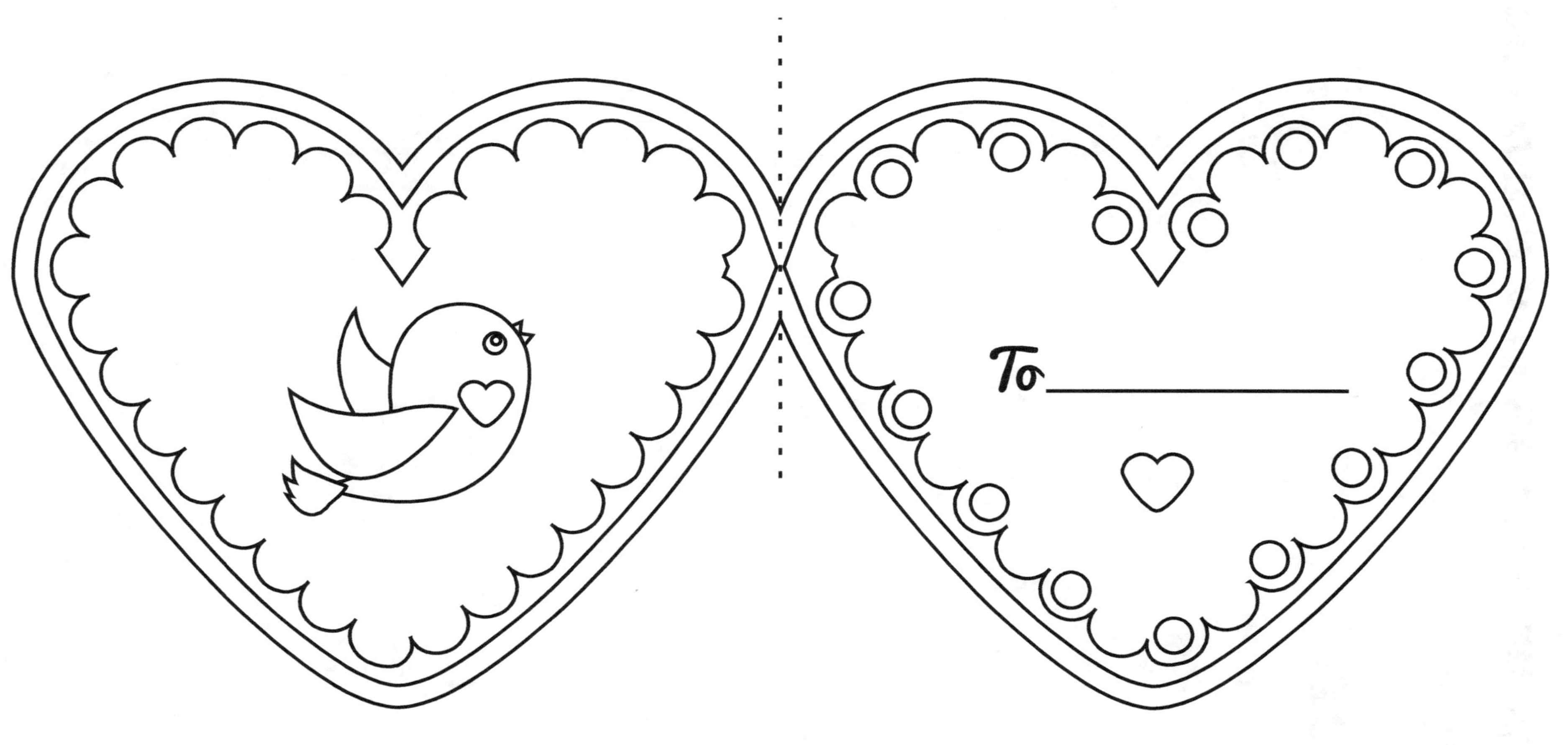

To

Take your time as you draw and color the bow.
4 GET
ME NOT!

Copy and color the picture

Connect the dots and color the rose.
LOVE YOU BUNCHES AND BUNCHES!

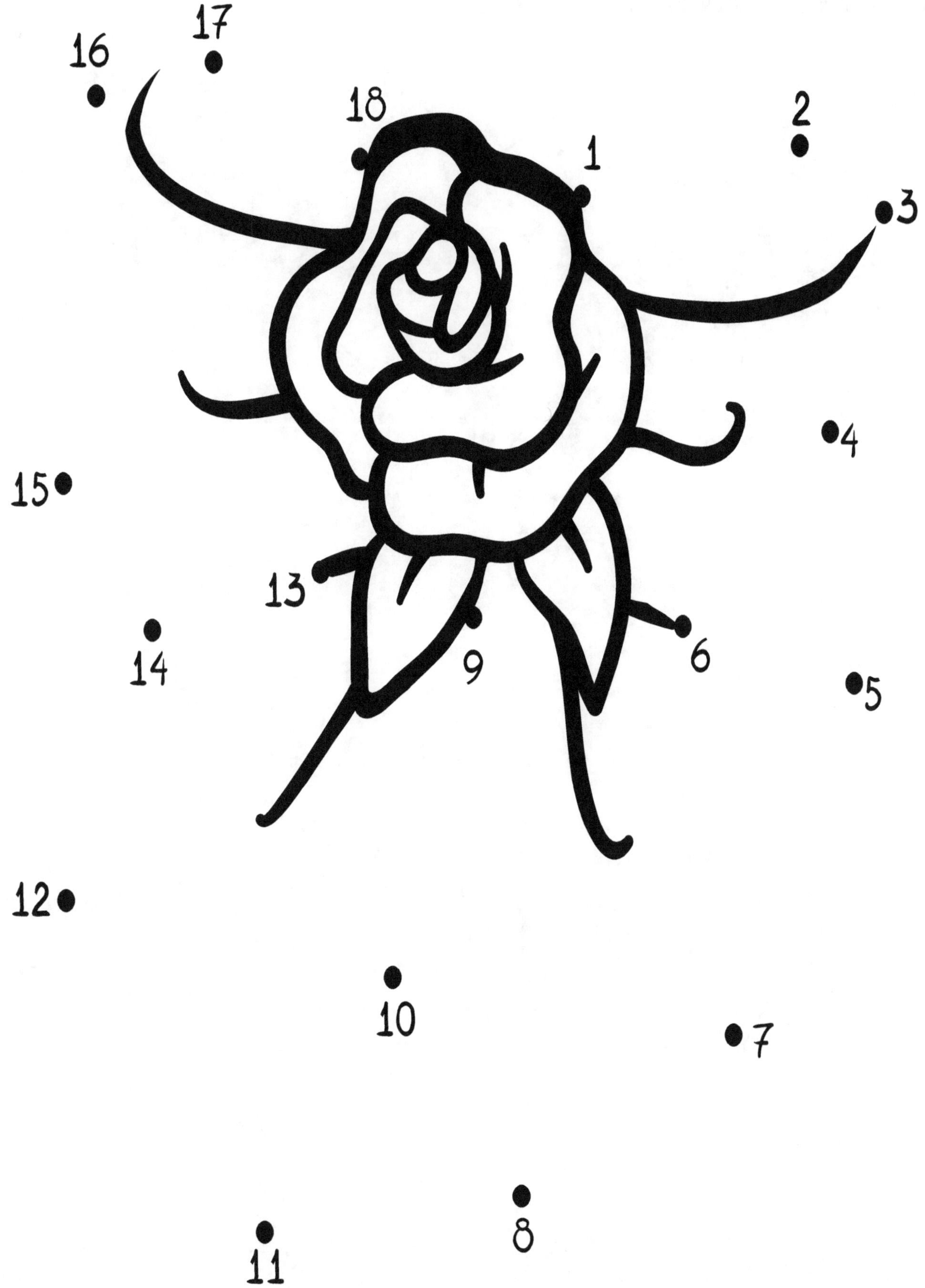

Which way to the cute cupid?
TO THE ONE I LOVE!

**Connect the dots and color it for your favorite valentine.
ALL MINE!**

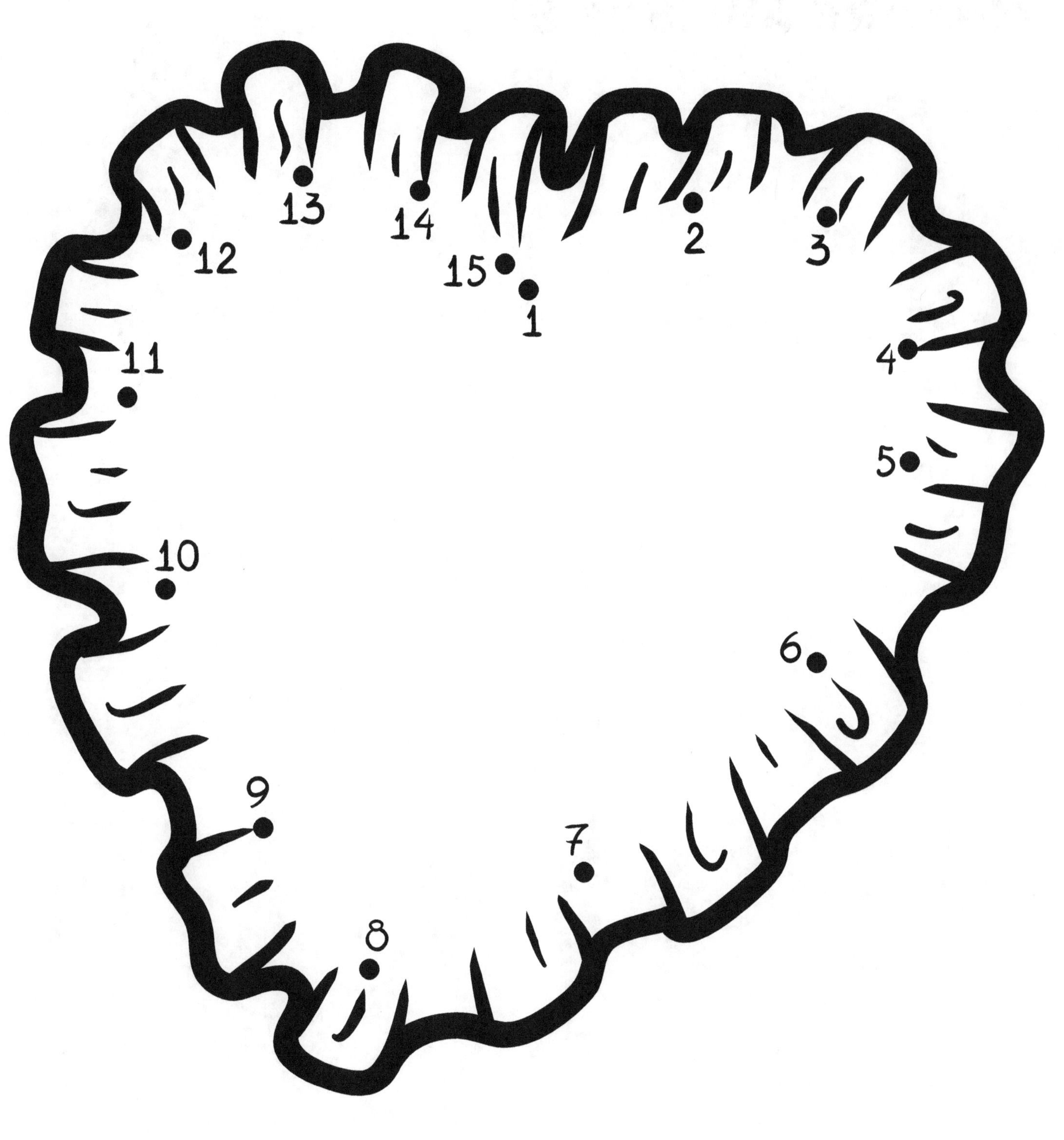

Can you match the picture to the shadows?
YOU ARE AWESOME!

Shadow Matching Game

- Color the pictures
- Draw the lines matching each picture to its shadow

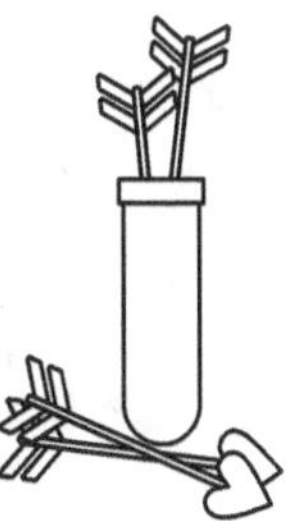   

Connect the dots.
YOU ARE SO LOVED!

Can you find the two identical hearts?
YOU ARE SO SMART!

Answer: _______________________

Connect the dots and color.
YOU ARE A SWEETHEART!

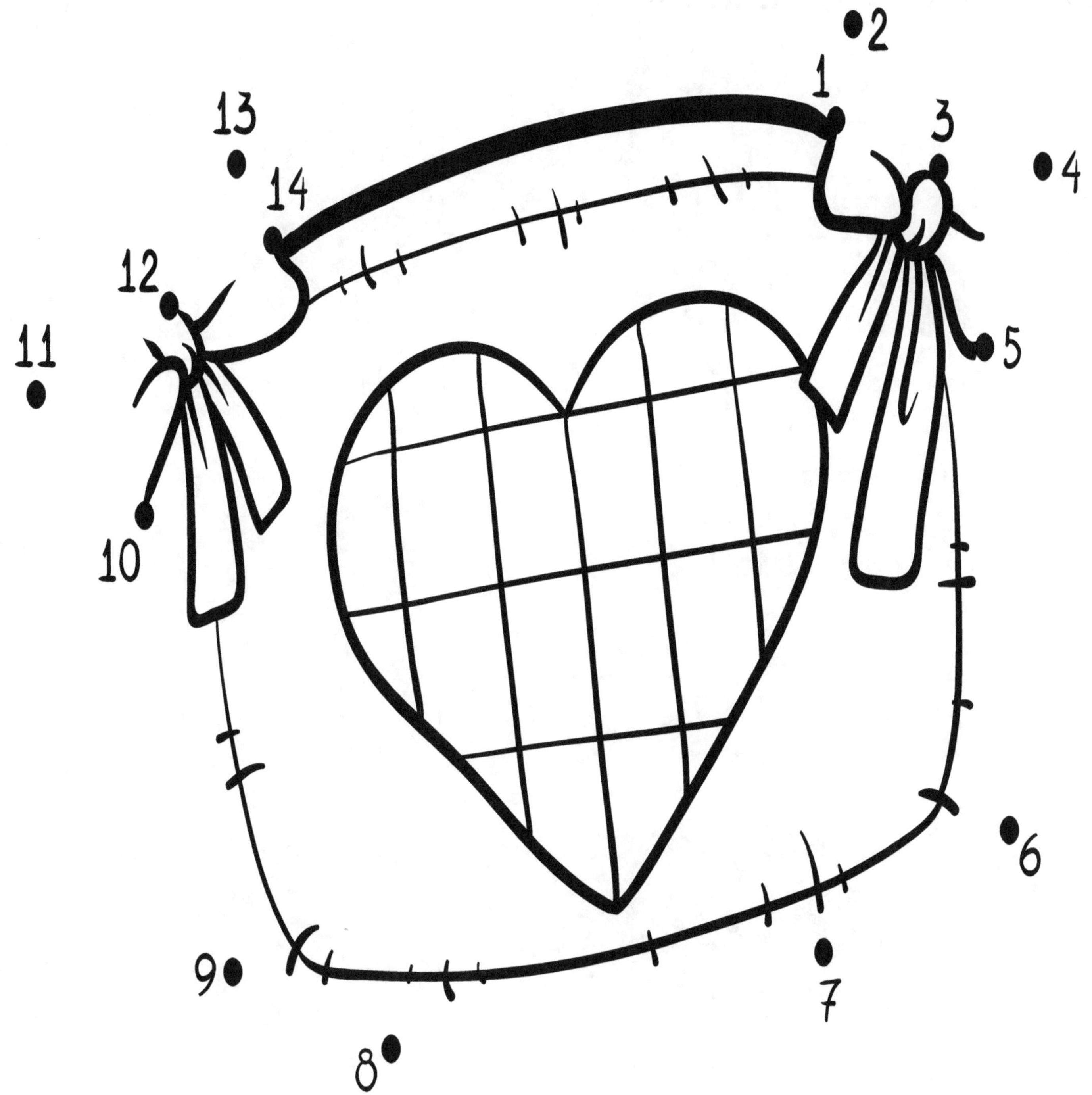

Count the objects carefully and circle the answer.
YOU ARE AMAZING!

Circle the right answer

9 8 7

4 5 6

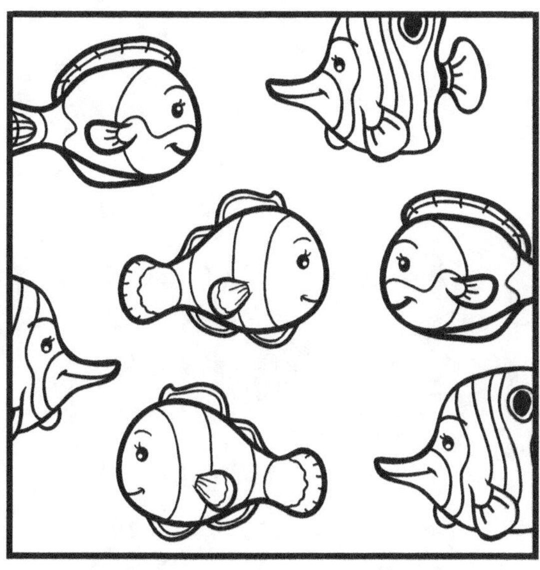

7 8 9

8 9 6

Help these sweethearts reach each other before Valentine's Day!
1/2 CUP OF HUGS
2 T. KISSES
4 cups of LOVE!

1. **Thing**
2. **Do**
3. **Words**
4. **You**

I LOVE YOU!

CHALLENGE: Can you make at least 20 words from the word valentine? (Hint: There's 198 possible words!)

1.

2.

3.

4.

5.

6.

7.

8.

9.

10.

11.

12.

13.

14.

15.

16.

17.

18.

19.

20.

**Connect the dots and color this cozy valentine scarf.
TOO CUTE!**

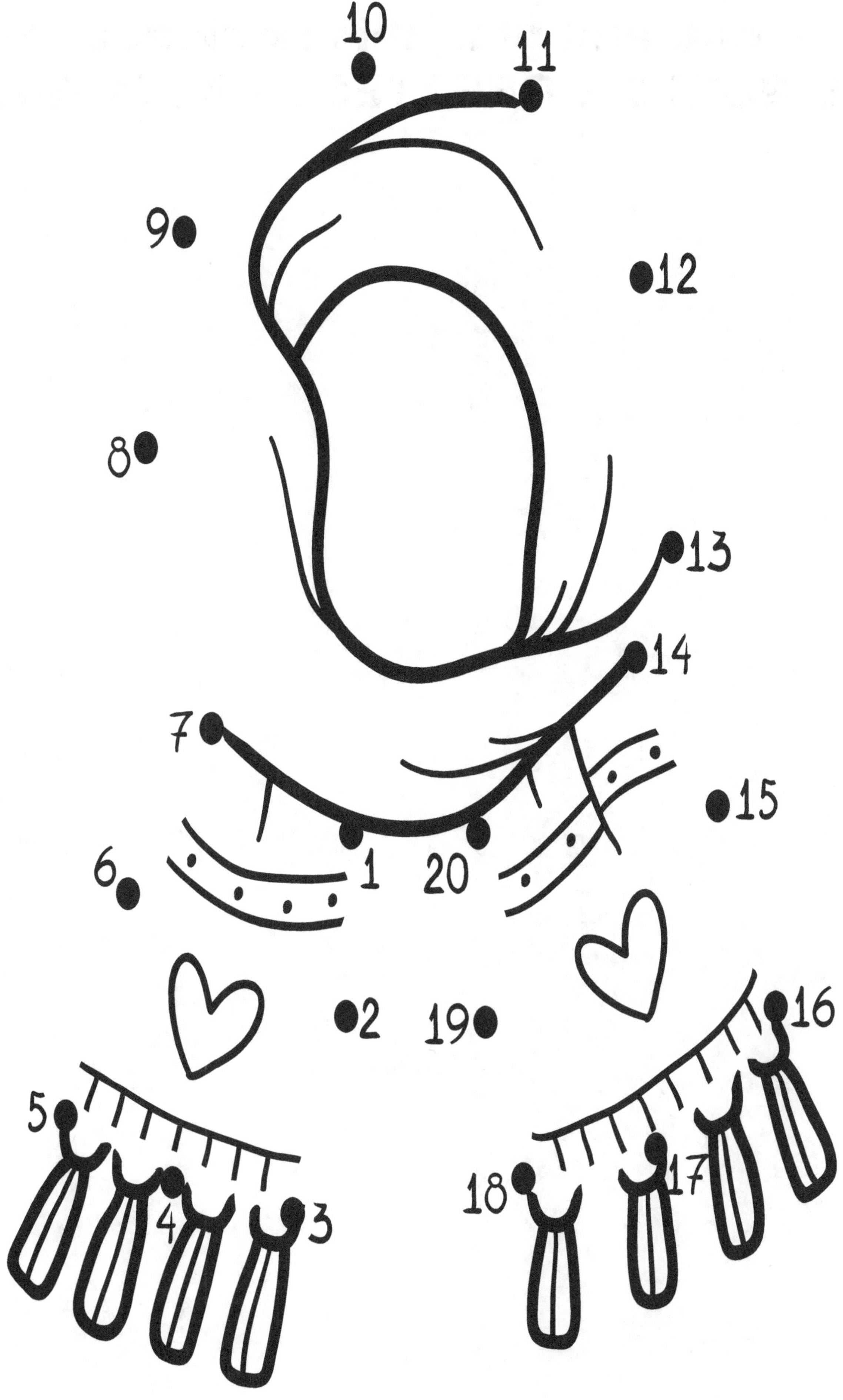

Color, cut, and glue this necklace for THE WORLD'S GREATEST VALENTINE!

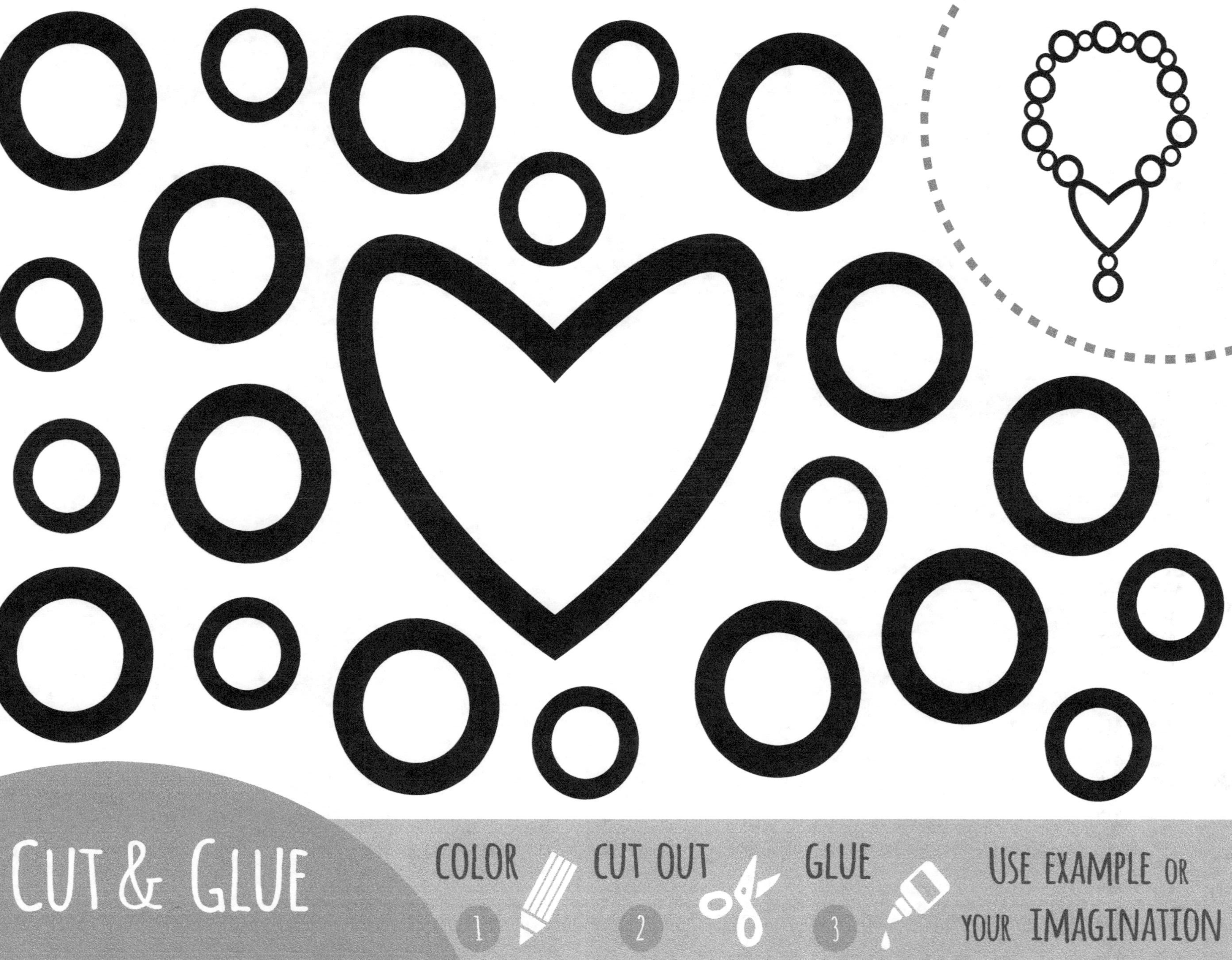
CUT & GLUE
COLOR
CUT OUT
GLUE
USE EXAMPLE OR
YOUR IMAGINATION
1
2
3

In FAIRY TALES, dreams come true...
I never thought I'd have a VALENTINE
as sweet as you!

Color the spaces with a dot!

**Stay warm as you complete the maze.
HEY BABY, IT'S COLD OUTSIDE!**

**YOU ARE MY SUN
YOU ARE MY MOON
AND ALL OF THE STARS!**

Valentine Activity Book Copyright 2018 by Florabella Publishing, LLC

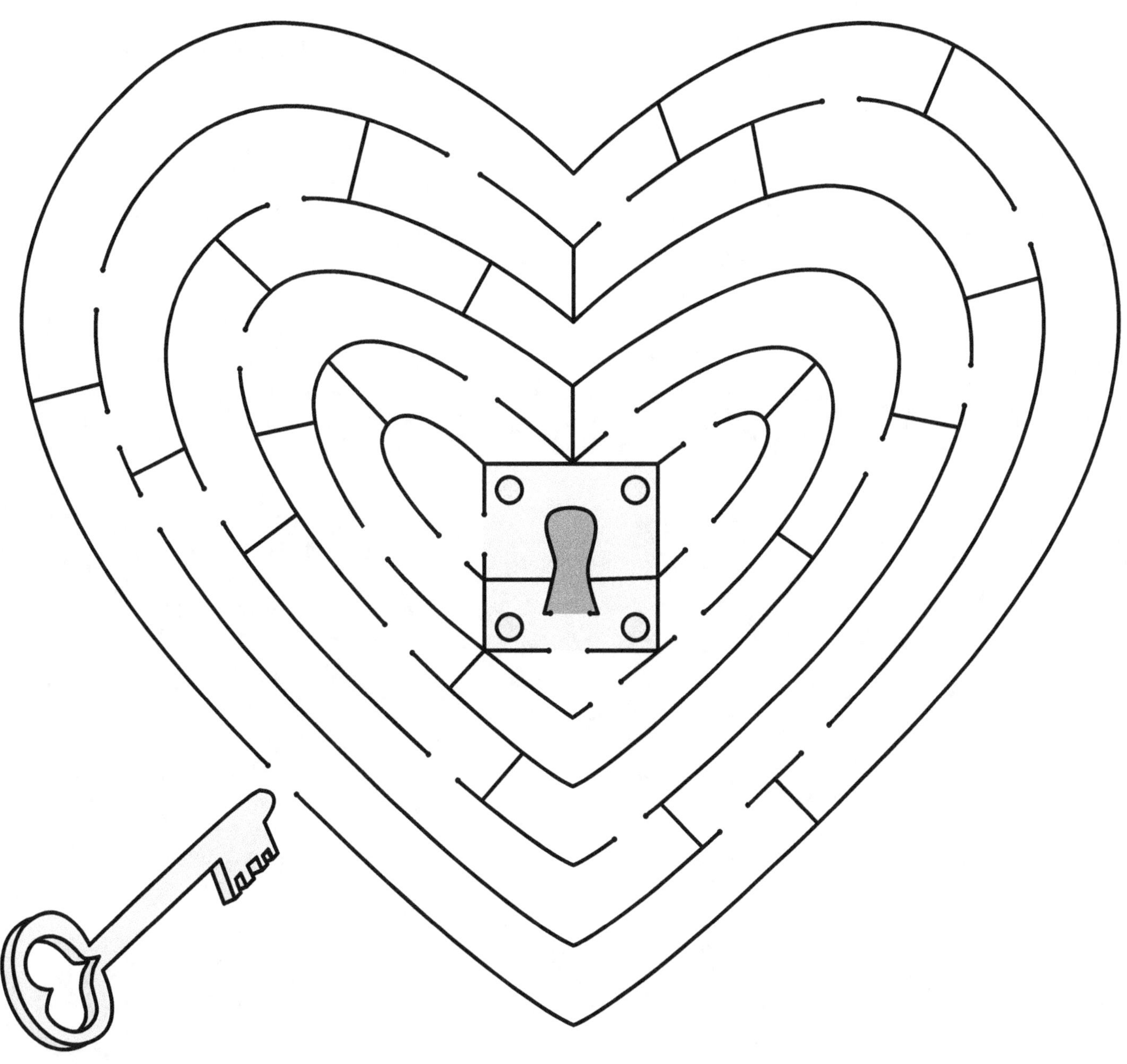

XOXO!

We hope you've enjoyed your Valentine's Day Activity Book. Thank you for your recent purchase!

FLORABELLA PUBLISHING.COM.

JUST HAD TO SEND YOU
A WISH FOR LOVE AND LAUGHTER!
HAPPY VALENTINE'S DAY!